Still Life

Still Life

Ciaran Carson

Wake Forest
University Press

First North American edition

For permission, write to
Wake Forest University Press
Post Office Box 7333
Winston-Salem, NC 27109
wfupress.wfu.edu

ISBN 978-1-930630-91-8
Library of Congress Control Number 2019950210

Designed and typeset by Nathan Moehlmann, Goosepen Studio & Press.

Still Life was first published by The Gallery Press in Ireland in 2019
and edited by Peter Fallon.

Publication of this book was generously supported by the Boyle Family Fund.

Contents

for Deirdre, Manus, Gerard, and Mary;
and for Caitlín, Pat, Breandán, and Liam

Claude Monet,
Artist's Garden at Vétheuil, 1880

Today I thought I'd just take a lie-down, and drift. So here I am
Listening to the tick of my mechanical aortic valve —
      overhearing, rather, the way
It flits in and out of consciousness. It's a wonder what goes on
      below the threshold.
It's quiet up here, just the muted swoosh of the cars on the
      Antrim Road,
And every so often the shrill of a far-off alarm or the squeal
      of brakes;
But yesterday some vandal upended the terracotta pot of
      daffodils
In our little front garden, that's not even as big, when I
      consider it,
As the double bed I'm lying on. Behind the privet hedge,
      besides the daffodils
There's pansies, thyme and rosemary. A Hebe bush. A laurel.
      Ruefully
I scuffed the spilled earth and pebbles with my shoe and
      thought of Poussin —
Was it Poussin? — and his habit of bringing back bits of
      wood, stones,
Moss, lumps of earth from his rambles by the Tiber; and the
      story of him

Reaching among the ruins for a handful of marble and
            porphyry chips
And saying to a tourist, 'Here's ancient Rome.' So, here's
            Glandore Avenue.

So different now from thirty years ago, the corner shop at
            the interface
Torched and the roadway strewn with broken glass and rubble.

There was something beautiful about the tossed daffodils all
            the same.
I'd never really taken them under my notice these past few
            difficult weeks.
It's late March, some of them beginning to turn and wilt and
            fade, heads
Drooping, papery at the tips, desiccated, or completely gone,
            reduced to calyx.
So many shades of yellow when you look at them. Gorse.
            Lemon. Mustard.
Honey. Saffron. Ochre. But then any word you care to mention
            has so many
Shades of meaning, and the flower itself goes under different
            names.
Narcissus. Daffadowndilly. Lent lily. So we wander down the
            road of what it is
We think we want to say. Etymologies present themselves,
            like daffodil
From asphodel—who knows where the *d* came from?—
            the flower

Of the underworld. They say it grows profusely in the meadows
of the dead,
Like a buttercup on its branching stem. And I see a galaxy of
buttercups in
A green field, and the yellow of the tall sunflowers in Monet's
Garden at Vétheuil
That flank the path where the woman and the two children
stand commemorated.

Strange how a smear of colour, like a perfume, resurrects
the memory
Of another, that which I meant to begin with. 'Asphodel, that
greeny flower.'

I'd just found the book I had in mind—*What Painting Is*
by James Elkins—
When the vandal struck. *Thud*. What the...? The gate clanged.
I looked out
The bay window to see a figure scarpering off down the street
to the interface...
What a book, though. I have it before me, open at this colour
plate, jotting notes
Into a jotter, which I'll work up later into what you're
reading now.
'The detail I'm reproducing here is a graveyard of scattered
brush hairs
And other detritus,' said Elkins. 'At the centre left, glazed over
by Malachite Green,

Are two crossed brush hairs, one of them bent almost at a
        right angle.
Just below them are two of Monet's own hairs, fallen into the
        wet paint.'
Brushstrokes laid down every which way. Jiggles. Jabs.
        Impulsive
Twists and turns. Gestures that 'depend on the inner feelings
        of the body,
And the fleeting momentary awareness of what the hand might
        do next.'
You listen to the body talking, exfoliating itself cell after cell.
        I saw it
Happening just now in the dust-motes drifting through this
        ray of sunlight.

So everything gets into the painting, wood-smoke from the
        studio stove,
The high pollen count of a high summer's day *en plein air* by
        the Seine.

The detail is so magnified it is impossible to tell what it is of,
        if you didn't,
Like Elkins, know. The visual field looks like a field. Shades
        of umber, khaki, mud,
And other greens beside the malachite. It could stand for
        anything it seems
In Monet's garden—or *Garden*, rather—as Poussin's handful
        of porphyry

Is Rome and of the days of the fall of Rome. I want it to go to
    the stately tune
Of a Poussin painting, *Landscape with a Man Washing His Feet
    by a Fountain,*
Say, where a woman sweeps by, balancing a basket on her head,
    and an old man
In blue dreams full-length on the grass. There are milestones
    and tombs,
And puddles on the road, and you can just imagine the
    whispering of the cistern.
A line of blue hills in the distance is contoured like a
    monumental sentence.
It's beautiful weather, the 30th of March, and tomorrow the
    clocks go forward.
How strange it is to be lying here listening to whatever it is
    is going on.
The days are getting longer now, however many of them I
    have left.
And the pencil I am writing this with, old as it is, will easily
    outlast their end.

Angela Hackett,
Lemons on a Moorish Plate, 2013

for Deirdre

We'd been talking about how back in the day we'd nothing
      much of anything,
Though what there was to wear—the uniform!—was too big.
      The sleeves
Drooped well below the fingertips. It gave you room to grow
      into. Years loomed.
Day after day, summer after summer, days were immeasurably
      longer then,
And the one tin bathful of hot water did the several children
      one after the other.
Then it seemed in no time at all you were into your teens.
      Because your birthday
Fell a week before Christmas—December the 18th—you'd have
      to make do
With the merest token of a family present. A set of bath salts,
      maybe, or a bar
Of lemon soap the simulacrum of a lemon, and we tried
      to remember
If such a thing came wrapped in tissue paper like the fruit
      itself, or was it
See-through cellophane? Then to summon up the names
      of yesteryear—

Yardley's April Violets; Mornay White Heather; Lenthéric
        Tweed! It's the 1960s,
And I see myself wondering what would be appropriate to buy
        for my mother,
Dazzled by the cornucopian Christmas window display of the
        chemist's shop.

All this, believe it or not, was apropos of Angela Hackett's
        painting—
Because when looking at a thing we often drift into a memory
        of something else,
However tenuous the link. Five years and more—ever since I
        bought it
For your birthday—it's been hanging on our bedroom wall,
        pleasing us
To look at it from time to time to see different things in it.
        Only now has it
Occurred to us to talk about or of it at this length, the lemons—
        three of them—
Proceeding in an anticlockwise swirl from pale lemon to a
        darker yellow
To an almost orange, tinged with green—degrees, we speculate,
        of ripeness
Or decay. You know how lemons, if left too long in the bowl,
        one or two from time
To time will show a blush of green, a dimple or a bruise of
        bluish green

That overnight becomes a whitish bloom? So we think Angela
                Hackett's lemons
Might be on the turn. Though it's possible the green tinge
                might be an echo
Of the two limes I haven't mentioned until now, nestled in
                against the lemons
On the indigo-and-white Moorish plate, all of which
                complicates the picture.

It gave us pause for thought. How long does it take, we
                wondered, for a lemon
To completely rot? We imagined a time-lapse film, weeks
                compressed into
Seconds, the lemon changing hue, developing that powdery
                bloom, then suddenly
Collapsing into itself to leave a shrunken, pea-sized, desiccated
                husk—the flesh
Evaporated, breathed into the atmosphere as it transpires.
                And that is why
On the 26th of March 2019 we set up the lemon experiment.
                On the avocado-and-aubergine-coloured
Moroccan saucer we bought in Paris we set a fresh lemon and
                a banana whose peel,
We are led to believe, releases ethylene gas and hence ripens
                any other fruit
With which it comes into contact. We wanted to see with
                our own eyes

The end of the life cycle of the lemon. I write this on the
            6th of April. The banana has gone
Black except at the tips. The lemon looks as fresh as ever.
            We've just been for our daily walk
Around the Waterworks. Ducks are kicking up a racket.
            A blackbird sings
From a blackthorn bush. And as we enter into Glandore from
            the Antrim Road
How clean and fresh and green are the newly sprung leaves
            of the chestnut tree!

Diego Velázquez,
Old Woman Cooking Eggs, 1618

The two eggs in the terracotta pot the *pièce de résistance*,
  albumen coagulating
Into solid white, fringes still diaphanous, shimmering—
  or is it
Simmering?—in oil or water, i.e. are they being fried or
  poached? That is
A question that has fascinated art historians for centuries.
  It reminds us,
Deirdre, of our sessions at the Atlantic Circle house back in
  the late 70s,
When we'd drink and smoke and play all night like there was
  no tomorrow—
Fiddles, flutes, Powers Gold Label whiskey, Gallaher's Blues
  cigarettes—then to rise
At noon and make the Ulster Fry (hangover cure *par excellence*)
  for six
Or seven of us, each with his or her own thinking as regards
  the egg: e.g.
Broken into oil so hot it's nearly smoking, so you get those
  crispy golden
Lacy edges, or basted gently, as these eggs by Velázquez
  seem to be.

I look it up in a book and find the painting is a *bodegón*—
  the cellar

Of a *bodega*, a tavern, where the commonplace of food, drink
and kitchenware
Is on display, and hence, in Spanish art, the term for 'still life'.
And then
I remember The Bodega bar in Belfast, the kind of place that
thought itself
A cut above the ordinary. Wrought-iron window grilles outside.
Dark interior —
It took your eyes a while to get accustomed to the gloom —
big sherry casks,
Fake wooden beams. I think a string of plastic onions. A Tio
Pepe ad.
It's 1973, and I'm pushing a pen in Family Income Supplements
behind the City Hall.
The IRA were bombing downtown shops and offices on a
weekly basis
It seems. My dreams are filled with wavering buildings,
avalanches of astonished
Glass. Now and then an alarm would sound and orderly the
clerks would proceed

Into the ordinary, glad cacophony of screeching jeeps and
klaxons wailing,
Freed for the day. So a trio of us would repair to The Bodega,
there to 'drink,
And leave the world unseen'. What did we talk about? Politics
I think not.
I know we shared a taste for literature. Faulkner, Lawrence,
Carlos Williams.

Joyce of course. And I was thinking of writing myself, I'd gone
        so far as to buy
A typewriter. What joy, to sit there in the chiaroscuro, round
        after round!
Every so often of an afternoon we'd hear a muffled thunder and
        the room
Would tremble, whiskey shiver in the glass. I dream I'm
        ordering another... there,
Behind the bar, where you'd expect a mirror, is the Velázquez.
        And I think,
How close to life, the texture of the blood red, papery
        dried red
Pepper pods! And then I think, but I knew nothing of
        Velázquez then.
And where are the two companions that for years I haven't
        thought of until now?

Jeffrey Morgan,
Hare Bowl, 2008

His gift revealed itself—a little book-sized still life of a bowl
        on a shelf—
Spongeware, 1850s—biscuit fired, says Jeffrey—decorated
        with a cut sponge,
A daisy chain of little blue flowers along the rim, and under
        them two hares
At full stretch running off to the right on the curve of the bowl.
        There'd be
Two others on the other side you can't see. Like the flowers,
        they're a faded blue, as is
The grass at their feet. Or is it shadow... When we think of the
        painted hares
We think of the hares that have entered our lives, however
        fleetingly.

The hare on the runway at Aldergrove airport, seen as you
        came into land.
The hare that crossed my path on the Milltown road, hedgerow
        to hedgerow in
The blink of an eye. The hare that stood and looked at us on
        Rathlin for an age.
The hare that you saw in your garden in Antrim, as tall as the
        child that you were.
So we go back to when we never knew each other, never
        dreaming then that we

Would end up in this here and now. We look at the *Hare Bowl*,
   then look at
Each other and smile. All day it draws us back to look at it,
   and look at it again.

That was then. This morning you've taken the bus into town
   to buy Easter eggs
And chocolates, and I'm left to contemplate the *Hare Bowl* on
   my own. It looks
Good upon the mantelpiece, propped beside the vase of
   daffodils we bought as
Tight green buds two days before, and now have opened up
   a blaze of yellow.
But I want to see the picture in a better light than this; the
   living room
It's in is dark, and the electric's always on. So I bring it to the
   parlour—facing south,
It gets the sun from dawn to dusk. I rest it on the back of the
   old overstuffed sofa

In the bay window. The muted colours suit the faded peachy
   pink of the fabric.
It's a few minutes after noon and the grey drizzle of earlier is
   lifting a little.
I raise the Venetian blind. A cool pearlescent light streams in.
   There are textures
In the painting that I hadn't seen before. The bowl itself is
   resting on

A terracotta-coloured shelf, little flecks of red in it, the left-hand
    corner of the edge
Signed 'J·M' in red. Discreet. You have to look for it. Then I want
    to talk about the bowl,
But I'm distracted trying to put words to the green of the wall
    it's placed against.

How many shades are mingled there from pear to sage to olive
    green? Now
That I look at it, is there a background hint of yellow? Then I
    notice the lemon
Of our experiment that's been occupying all this time in the
    parlour on
Its Moroccan saucer. We binned the banana when it went
    black. As for the lemon,
It's ever so slightly beginning to shrink and wizen, but still
    holding firm after
Three weeks — firmer in fact than fresh. In any event it glows
    against the green
Of the wall, the earth of the shelf, and the blue and creamy
    white of the bowl.

I'm wondering how Jeffrey got that illusionistic craquelure
    effect. So I email him;
He emails back. 'With the surface all wet and with a small
    Winsor & Newton
No. 7 sable brush (these are still licked into shape by old
    women — what happens when

They die—that's it) I paint the craquelure directly into the wet
        paint, then
Go to eat and watch *Newsnight*—it takes a week to dry.' A car
        horn sounds.
I look out the window. It's the usual crowded parking, morning
        surgery hours—
The Antrim Road Medical Centre is only five doors up Glandore
        Avenue from us.

I'm often there. *Was* there earlier this morning, getting an
        advance blood
For tomorrow's treatment at the City. In fact we're waiting to be
        seen there now.
The neutrophils are up to par, so everything is good to go. Here
        comes the nurse
With the cannula trolley. She ties the ligature, palps my lower
        arm to find a vein,
Then, head down, that look of utter concentration—Vermeer's
        Lacemaker—
As delicately, slowly, she works the needle in. *Cannula* the Latin
        for a little reed,
Or maybe a pen—the needle a nib with chemo ink to overwrite
        the faulty DNA.

Ninety minutes later we're out of the hospital. You call Fonacab,
        90333333,
You remember when we called it the Five 3s? Forty years ago
        or more...

The city centre's gridlocked, according to the cabbie—an
          ambulance wails by—
Says he'll try the Westlink—we pass the Royal, where four
          years ago
I had my cardiac procedure—triple bypass, mechanical aortic
          valve—at last we
Reach the Antrim Road: past the Waterworks, and all the
          cherries suddenly
In bloom! And we're both so looking forward to seeing Jeffrey
          Morgan's *Hare Bowl* again.

Paul Cézanne,
The Stove in the Studio, c. 1865

Since I saw it first in 1993 how often have I thought of
    Cézanne's studio stove
And the great big potbellied cast-iron black cauldron sitting
    squat on its top,
With God-knows-what seething away in its belly, or sweet
    nothing's in the pot,
And the back of a canvas on a pinewood stretcher propped face
    to the wall
Behind the stove perhaps to dry, or not; and, hard to figure from
    the chiaroscuro,
A little painting, or an artist's palette; and that tiny palette,
    would it be a sketch;
And a pottery pot on the floor; and another dim something in
    the tiny room, all
Lit by the glow of a single red coal in the jaws of the coal-black
    cast-iron stove?

Nicolas Poussin,
Landscape with a Calm, 1650–51

For a long time, if only now and then, I'd idly think about
      the difference
Between 'hawthorn' and 'blackthorn'—were they indeed
      divergent genera,
Or merely synonymous terms for the same plant?—invariably
      deferring
The quest until, my conscience pricked by the blackbird I'd
      put in my poem
Of a fortnight ago to sing from a blackthorn for the sake of
      consonance, I resolved
To settle the matter for once and for all. So I googled it.
      Blackthorn, flowers first,
Then leaves; hawthorn, leaves first, then flowers. I remembered
      the tree as
Sprinkled by a hail of tiny blossoms. Not a leaf to be seen.
      The wood was dark. Cautiously
I put my finger to a thorn: it was needle-sharp and hard.
      Was this
The thorn that cut one to the quick? I put the question to
      one side.

For I've been thinking of the stanza as an ample room I want
      to wander in: Latin
Stantia, present participle of *stare*, to stand, hence Italian *stanza*,
      a room, a place wherein

You stand; a stopping place, a station. Of the poem as a
        verbal suite
Of interconnecting rooms—here, I'm entering the virtual
        London National Gallery tour,
Important portals with massive architraves of blue-grey
        striated marble that
Successively invite you into spaces you can walk right through
        or dawdle in
To contemplate a phrase, the line or contour of a painting,
The happenstance of a statue. And it occurs to me that our
        habitual journeys
To the Waterworks might form such a measure, as we
        sometimes scan this memorable
Place or that, and dwell on it a while as we have many
        unremembered times before.

For now, we're on the Antrim Road. It's Easter Sunday and the
        sun is shining.
We take the usual turn at Hopefield Avenue. Here No. 1 once
        stood. It was
A beautiful house back then. We'd peep over the privet hedge
        to peer into it.
A Chinese vase in the bay window. A landscape on the parlour
        chimney breast.
Now a waste ground. Chain-link fencing. We pause here to
        visualize once more
The goldfinch we saw two years ago, perched on a thistle-head,
        plucking fluff

For food. Then to circumvent the House of Cerberus, the
        chained watchdog
That lies in a circle of its own excrement. We are glad to reach
        the House of Kids,
The front garden a jumble of primary colours: red, blue, yellow;
        toy dump truck,
Wheelbarrow, JCB; green garden hose, bucket & spade, and
        green garden gnome.

And so to the Waterworks. We cross the road and enter by the
        little Eastern Gate.
We take our customary anticlockwise circuit across Milewater
        Bridge, left into
Bird Alley: a tall impenetrable hawthorn hedge on one side—
        just beginning to bloom!—
And a minor Everglades of willow on the other. Birdsong
        surrounds us,
The trees reverberant with trills and warbles. Gradually we
        enter a new acoustic:
Here comes Squawk Island, a place so densely wooded that its
        denizens are not
To be seen, but loudly heard in their cacophony of panic-
        stricken shrieks
And squeals. But soon we'll be arriving at our usual bench,
        where we'll be well
Out of earshot. Now we sit to contemplate the water, whether
        calm or ruffled.
Here we reflect on all we've seen throughout the years, and all
        there is to come.

And so we come to talk of how we take our bearings from
       the moment
Of a painting, where everything is at a standstill. Poussin's
       Calm. For some time past
The landscape of the Waterworks had made me think of his.
       His lake, our pond.
On the Cavehill Road the skyline of serried chimneypots
       accorded to the crenellated
Battlements of his citadel. Extending the conceit, sunlit
       rectangles,
Parallelograms and cubes of shade, roofs, bay windows,
       apertures began
To correspond. The yellow gable of a terrace house took on
       a new significance—
See that other patch of yellow—there, below the citadel?
       I looked at
Reproductions, images from books, the internet. The more
       you looked
The more there was to see to know exactly what there was,
       and what was not.

For there is more to it than meets the eye. But first, an overview.
       It measures
Some three feet by four. A generous picture. A great citadel
       takes up the centre.
A colossal twin-cragged mountain stands to its left. Clouds
       hang in a sky
The blue of the pellucid lake that occupies the middle ground.
       On its further shore

A long drove of sheep and cattle. In the foreground a goatherd
        tends his goats.
These are some of the most immediately apparent features of
        the landscape.
I think it takes us a while to get the horse galloping off stage
        right, urged on
By its bareback rider, for it's dark over there in the shadow
Of the framing tree. And what's this curious structure that it
        dashes past? Seemingly
A washhouse—look, there's a woman leaning over a trough,
        and another horse drinking from it.

For one thing leads to another, as the heads of the unruly
        goats point
This way and that, directing us to look further. That fire in
        the middle distance,
What is it for? And what about the lake, that neither crag nor
        cloud are mirrored in it?
As for the citadel, a piece of its intricate structure appears
        missing from its
Reflection. Regarding the Grecian frieze of animals, why is the
        bull of the herd
Not recapitulated? And now—as musicians, we should have
        seen this before—
Look at the bagpiper bringing up the rear of the drove, about to
        break into tune!
Look at his cap, tunic, pannier, belt, pipe and drone, etcetera,
        his complex stoop

And stride into the lateral flow and the light. He drives or
        follows the entablature
Of animals into the time of day, whatever it might be. And we
        follow him.

For music is afoot, and we imagine it from what we know of
        music, tunes
Reiterated over decades, played in back rooms, or upon the
        stanza of a stage.
Melodies that alter between hearing and remembering,
        remembering
The friends we learned them from. Missing bits we
        touchingly get
Wrong, yet somehow work. How many the utterances of
        The Blackbird, each one
Different from the last? And again I hear the mad cadenza
        of the blackbird in his tree.
The bellows groan and creak, the piper starts up, windblown
        skirl and parp
Encouraging the beasts into a great polyphony of pastorale.
        Lowing, bleating,
Undulating to the groundswell of the drone, moving slowly
        in the amplitude—
The musician driving the stock-still moment steadily into
        the future.

Joachim Patinir,
Landscape with Saint Jerome, 1516–17

For some weeks afterwards Poussin's 'handful of porphyry'—
    more accurately,
According to Giovanni Bellori, 'a little earth and gravel, with
    fragments
Of porphyry (*minuzzoli di porfidi*) and marble crushed almost
    to a powder'—kept
Weighing in my mind; but lightly, almost palpable as dust.
    What could it be?
I went to sleep on it, and woke at dawn with the word *cloud*
    in my head—
'Any kind of mass formed by agglomeration, cumulus', cognate
    with *clod* and *clot*,
'A lump of solid or coherent matter'. Hence the obsolete
    construction of a cloud,
'A mass of rock, a hill'. I'd been dreaming on a mountainside
    beside a faery thorn
When she herself appeared to me and breathed these words
    into my ear.

Ding-dong! That was the doorbell. I'd been writing away at this,
    and momentarily
It put me in mind of the carriage return bell of my old Imperial
    typewriter, how

Back in the 80s I measured my verse by the width of an A4
        page. For whatever reason
I've gone back to that arbitrary rule that turns your thinking
        unexpectedly. Though
Necessarily it turns out differently when printed in a book.
        The parameters are
Narrower. The line breaks change, and drop a hemistich.
        So the landscape
Format of the stanza radically changes shape, becoming more
        like a tree
Or a shrub with a dense central trunk—arboreal, in other
        words, like these
Which you are viewing now, which I have written only now.

But let me pick up from the happenstance: it was the postman
        at the door, with
A large packet from France. On the *Déclaration en Douane*
        was written
Brochure Livre. What could it be? I unwrapped it. *Patinir ou
        l'harmonie du monde.*
Then I remembered. Weeks ago I'd sent my Monet's Garden
        poem to the painter
Clement McAleer. And, apropos of Poussin, he'd emailed this:
        'Another painter
Who brought in rocks, pebbles and moss to stimulate the
        imagination
For landscape composition was Joachim Patinir.' So I'd ordered
        Patinir. Le voilà!

The cover was a landscape with towering crags. I turned to the
            inner flap,
Whose first sentence read: *Roc et ciel, Patinir a trouvé sa formule
            et sa devise.*

'Rock and sky, Patinir realized his formula and watchword.'
            I open the book
At the first plate. *Paysage avec saint Jérôme.* There he is, the
            picture of austerity,
In a lean-to built against a freakish jagged monolith of flint,
            drawing the thorn
From the paw of his emblematic lion. And, half-hidden by a
            pillar of his shack,
There's the single book that answers to his status as the patron
            of translators. Off
To the right a boy leads a blind man down a path, and
            another lion—
Rampant, evidently wild—threatens a muleteer. What
            could it be
In those panniers? Perhaps he is a travelling colourman
            with his wares
Of indigo, malachite, madder lake, Naples yellow, *terre verte*,
            and orpiment.

No doubt he is bound for the monastery that dwells upon a
            plinth of rock
Below those prodigious molar crags. The scriptorium
            is renowned

Throughout Christendom for its illumination of the Word.
         Also of interest
To the pilgrim is the lapidarium, where one may contemplate
         the meaning
Of the world, as illustrated by the various types of stone:
         such as earths,
Salts and nitres; marine stones, including sponges, corals,
         and the Halcyon Stone;
Stones engendered in animals, including bezoar, stag's tears,
         toad-stone, and pearls;
Stones in the shape of animals and plants; and marbles.
         Chief among the latter
Is the purple-veinèd porphyry, emblem of the grandeur that
         was Rome.

In the background, under a sky of mountain and cloud,
         the ships in the bay
Are bringing in loads of language. Excisemen of the Custom
         House take out the words,
Weigh them, measure their specific gravity and, ascertaining
         their significance,
Give them their due. As for Jerome, do not be fooled by the look
Of this barelegged greybeard in a hair shirt, crucifix and skull
         before him; he is
Their secret master. He has written loads of books, and there
         are more to come.
I fancy his head is full of verbal murmuration. Sometimes
         innumerable birds

Settle in his tree to sing. Sometimes they bring themselves
        into the realm
Where rock and sky collaborate, to vanish in a cloud
        of porphyry.

William Nicholson,
Ballroom in an Air Raid, 1918

The weather has taken a turn. Thick cloud cover, impending
          rain. It makes you consider
What it must be like to be the occupant of the sub-cloud car—
          a small device
Shaped something like a bomb, with an open cockpit,
          stabilizing fins and a rudder
At the rear. Consider it being lowered from the bomb bay of
          a Zeppelin at the end of
A 3,000-foot cable attached to a winch—the airship cruising
          safely out of sight
Inside a cloud bank while the crewman aboard the sub-cloud
          car, dangling some
Hundreds of feet under the clouds, directs the bombing via
          a telephone.
Consider the look, the weight, the layered textures of his outfit:
          thick woollen
Long underwear; standard blue flight coveralls; leather overalls;
          felt overshoes over
A pair of standard boots; leather gloves lined with sheep's wool;
          a lined helmet
With goggles; and a scarf. Consider London with its domes,
          theatres, temples; consider its skies.

Now consider William Nicholson's *Ballroom in an Air Raid*—
        no ballroom
In actuality, but the two-storey Masonic Temple located in the
        sub-basement
Of the Piccadilly Hotel. Such a cavernous space, concourse
        or antechamber
To the Underworld. Consider the rolled-up red carpet snaking
        from one end
Of the floor to the other that is a dark portal. Figures emerging
        from or loitering
Before it, some of them more shadow than discernible. Others
        aimless. Two
Stand out as officers by the cut of their cloth and their stance
        but ill at ease.
A stray chair stands at an odd angle. A woman sits on the carpet
        with a small child
Face down in her lap. A baby lies on the carpet in front of you.
        Two women sit
In the corner, each with a baby in her lap. One of them looks
        out at you,
The viewer. Consider the dirigible indiscernible in the bank
        of cloud above Piccadilly.

Canaletto,
The Stonemason's Yard, c. 1725

Here we are again at the waste ground of 1 Hopefield Avenue,
          and behind
The chain-link fencing is a big yellow JCB emblazoned
          McNABNEY BROS
That wasn't there yesterday; where we saw the goldfinch
          two years ago,
Perched feeding on a thistle-head. Weeds have been culled,
          rubble levelled,
Trenches dug in preparation for whatever. An apartment block?
          If so, for how much
Longer will the gable wall of No. 3 be visible? It had passages
          of inexplicable brickwork
We liked to try to make something of, to say nothing of the
          ghost of the chimney flue of No. 1—

The kind of thing that had I been a painter I'd have liked to put
          into a painting—
I can see a landscape by Tony Swain, where mountains, chairs,
          windows, meadows,
Lighthouses, graffiti, trees, sand dunes, power stations
          intermingle, offering
The viewer many potential routes through a sometimes
          considerable length

Of scenery. Take for instance the boats, the jetty, the sweeping
        path to the volcano,
The chapel on the hill. Sometimes some words of the print of
        the newspaper support
Are left visible, though more often than not they are veiled or
        totally obscured.

Typically, his day starts with a read of the newspaper.
        The Guardian, specifically.
He scans for things he might use between reading and
        looking until
Something, whether photograph or text, engages him —
        an area of brickwork, say, or of
Repeated prepositions. So he pulls out the page, thinks, and
        paints something on
The something on the page; thinks again, paints again. He
        likes the way newspaper
Gets wrinkled and puckered when painted on, and gives
        what's been obliterated
Incidental texture. Thing after thing he follows what he thinks
        they want to become.

Seeing I take *The Guardian*, I think I'll try that too. See where
        it takes me.
So this morning—the 11th of May 2019—I open the paper at
        random at a feature
On the Venice Biennale, where I read about Julie Mehretu,
        'whose paintings

Often use newspaper images as their source, but overpainted ...
    so that
Their original material becomes obscured'. I take this as a
    favourable omen to write
Toward Venice, in the form of Canaletto's *The Stonemason's Yard*,
    a picture
I'd been always taken by. From now on I can take it as a
    palimpsest to write upon.

And what a different take on Venice is *The Stonemason's Yard*
    from the standard
Canaletto Grand Tourist view: those magnificent regattas on
    the Grand Canal—
Golden pageantry, the gorgeous barges and the glittering
    palazzi—no, this is
Almost Dutch, attentive to the everyday, the seemingly
    authoritative title a misnomer:
The view is of the Campo San Vidal, the 'yard' a temporary
    set-up for the repair of
The nearby church (not seen in the picture) of San Vidal,
    though on Google Maps it lies immediately
Behind the viewer. The church across the canal—it is indeed
    the Grand Canal!—

Is that of Santa Maria della Carità, whose campanile collapsed
    on 17th March 1744
And was never rebuilt. I'm thinking what a clatter the bells
    must have made

As they fell, when suddenly, the *ting-ting* of your incoming
Fonacab 'taxi dispatched' text!
I close the laptop. Twenty minutes later we're in the waiting
room. It takes an hour
Before we're seen, but now I'm seated in the La-Z-Boy recliner,
hooked up
To the drip: a 1115ml infusion over 60 minutes. I've brought
along a little Thames
And Hudson Canaletto pocket book by Antonio Paolucci to
pass the time.

I look at it from time to time. There's an LED display with a
digital countdown on
The trolley but I have to look over my shoulder for it. In any
event it issues
An almost inaudible murmur I imagine measuring the chemo
trickling down...
Dozing a little, I hear it entering my ear canal... *cannula,*
cannula, Canaletto, Cunaletto...
I open my eyes and there you are, looking at me. I say, Can you
get the Muji pen
And notebook from my jacket pocket? And write this down?
You do. *My writing hand*
Is out of action due to the cannula in the wrist through which the
chemo flows.

The LED begins to flash and beep. Chemo's nearly over, just
00.05 on the clock, then

We're out. But first I have to pee! The chemo fairly makes you
        go. Now much relieved
And in the taxi home, I'm looking at the picture in the pocket
        book. Barely three
Inches by four, but what a world of characters and things
        implying time—the gondoliers
Who ply their measured pole from quay to quay; the time it
        takes for the distaff woman
On the balcony to spin a length of yarn; or for the stooping
        woman to draw
Water from the well. As for the workmen chipping away amid
        the rubble at the marble

Bit by bit—see how the white stone is reflected by the high,
        dazzling bell tower
In the background to the right—are they paid by piece or by
        time? From the shadows
Cast it looks like mid-morning. How long is it since the cock
        first crew—there,
Perched resplendent on that window sill, looking east from
        the left of the frame?
The two lines of washing on the far bank, will they be dry by
        noon? The pot plants
On an upper balcony, in what sequence planted? Over
        everything and everyone
The bell-strokes of the campanile of Santa Maria della Carità
        proclaim the proper time.

Then there is the deep time of the City of Venice, floating on
        sleech on a city of stilts.
The stone, how long did it take to quarry and ship from
        Istria to here,
To say nothing of its archaeology? Paint layers at another end
        of the temporal spectrum:
Now I'm looking on the internet at this magnified 400x
        cross-section sample
Of a microscopic flake of terracotta building: lead white, red
        and orange ochres,
Naples yellow, red lake, and some black. A scintilla of Venetian
        sky: lead white,
Vermilion, Prussian blue and yellow earth. The Prussian blue
        has faded over time—

Everything infused by time and marble dust! But look at
        the toddler in the foreground who,
Fallen backwards on his bottom, has just released this elegant,
        sparkling arc of pee!
His mother commiserates; he'd been doing so well at the
        staggering toward her
Open arms. He'll learn in time how many steps to take before
        whatever end
He had in mind; and I, however long it takes to write this
        poem, whatever it might be.
For here we are again in Hopefield, looking through the green
        chain-link fencing
At the big yellow JCB. And as for what they're going to build
        there, we can't wait to see.

John Constable,
Study of Clouds, 1822

'The sound of water escaping from mill dams, etc., willows,
     old rotten planks,
Slimy posts and brickwork, I love such things,' said Constable.
     Also, trees and wind
And clouds reflected in the water, as shown by his limpid
     Water-meadows at Salisbury.
His father owned watermills and windmills; he understood
     weather from childhood.
Of hail squalls in spring he had this to say: 'The clouds
     accumulate in very large masses,
And from their loftiness seem to move but slowly; immediately
     on these large clouds
Appear numerous opaque patches, which are only small clouds
     passing rapidly
Before them. Those floating much nearer the earth may
     perhaps fall in with
A stronger current of wind, which drives them with greater
     rapidity from light to shade
Through the lanes of the clouds; hence they are called by
     wind-millers and sailors, *Messengers*,
And always portend bad weather.' Therefore Constable learned
     the craft of chiaroscuro.

Ten years ago it was your going through what had to be gone
        through. First the little blip,
Then the bigger blip. We'd scan the clouds for whatever augury
        they bore, clouds
That bloom and dim from marble sheen to darks of silver at the
        edges, in the throes of being
And becoming. Shown what showed on the screen, we
        wondered, what do we know of
Our bodies, the internal country undiscovered until now,
        and then not understood? Now
It has befallen me to go through what will be, we gaze into
        the clouds and listen to the sound
Of water in the Waterworks... I open a book to see what
        Constable recorded one day on
Hampstead Heath: '31st Sepr 10–11 o'clock morning looking
        Eastward a gentle wind to the East'—
The moving cumulus caught on the fly between hand and eye?
        Study, as in 'an act of learning'?
Let's say a happenstance of Constable and cloud, the final
        picture uninterpretable—
Quasi-shapely, cauliflower-plump, with just a hint of dark
        top right to prove the chiaroscuro.

Nicolas Poussin,
Landscape with the Ashes of Phocion, 1648

Let me begin by writing about the instrument I'm writing
      with: a 'Lady Patricia'
Mechanical — 'retractable' or 'clutch' — pencil made in the USA
      by Waterman in 1931,
In a translucent 'onyx' celluloid, somewhat dimmed with age,
      but still beautiful to look at,
White peach marble with feint hints of amber and terracotta
      veins. Feminine, slighter counterpart
To the heftier, senatorial 'Patrician', it suits my hand fine as
      I write, or scribble, rather,
Standing at the bedside dressing-table; and it's still strange
      to me that I do so.
Before the diagnosis I'd written nothing publishable for four
      years, but when I took
The pencil up it seemed to set me free. Before that, I'd drafted
      poems with a Muji pen,
And still do on occasion; years before that, vintage fountain
      pens, of which the pencil
Is a spin-off, one half of a pen and pencil set I picked up
      for a song on eBay.

8th June. It's two a.m. the morning after my last chemo of
      the cycle. Can't sleep. Steroids
They give you to get you through, they make me sketch and jot.
      Flickers to be

Amplified tomorrow into more coherent form, not
        reproduction — much on my mind
Regarding paintings. For all the painter draws, the viewer
        draws conclusions, repro after
Reproduction of the *Ashes*, seeing things in them perhaps not
        there at all, perhaps not
Seeing what there is, not ever having seen the thing itself.
        I might easily have glimpsed it
In the Walker Gallery Liverpool, where I was once, and had
        gone to look at it, but I knew nothing
Then of Poussin, and had I come to it, it likely would have been
        invisible to me.

Yet the view is an imaginary one, of an Ancient Greek city state,
        the city of Megara:
Poussin's illustration to a story. But more of that anon. Let us
        look at the city as it
Appears, as described by Tom Lubbock: 'A row of massive oaks,
        heavy with foliage,
Runs right across the foreground. It's a high natural wall
        planted alongside the actual
Low wall, a great shady barricade. But it has an opening.
        These guardian trees
Frame the city like a pair of curtains or wings. A road runs
        between them, coming
From outside. Bracketed by the dark trees the luminous city
        appears beyond, a composition
Of arches, pillars, squares, rectangles, diagonals — buildings
        that suggest a set

Of toy bricks... Megara has a structure. It's ruled by a centre
        and a hierarchy.
The façade of the classical temple looks out at us, pretty well
        from the middle.

'It is the face of the city, the focal point of the whole scene.
        But this temple is not the culmination.
Standing behind, there is a great wooded rock, its two jagged
        molar stumps emerging from
The vegetation covering its base.' The kind of writing you need
        to copy out
To properly infuse its cadences of assonance into your system:
        'row, oaks, foliage,
Foreground, low, opening'—O what lovely open O's! And then
        the E's: 'these, trees,
Between, trees, appears'. Musically enthused, you read the piece
        aloud as if
The words were truly yours in all their salient particularity.
        Or should we, given
Poussin's words—'*Moi, qui fait profession des choses muettes*'—
        thereof remain silent?

Or Wittgenstein's, 'What can be shown, cannot be said.' No,
        we scribble and gabble. And yet,
As our eye is drawn into the sunlit arena in front of the temple,
        we imagine an acoustic.
Here are dotted Poussin's trademark miniature figures,
        walking, talking, playing music.

Archers going *whoosh!* and *thwock!* to hit the target. Bathers
         laugh and splash.
Listen then to what you see, you hear it as a great orchestral pit.
         And only now
Do I spot the tiny white streak of a far-off shirt being taken
         off—it strikes the ear
Like the lightning *ting!* of a triangle, the chime of an antique
         clock, or a music box,
The movement of Subbuteo figures synchronized upon a table
         top. Meanwhile, temple,
Rock and cloud compose a pyramid from ground to sky to loom
         above and overlook
The open field. I take a closer look, and take my pencil up to jot
         a note when *drat!* The lead

Just broke. I shake it and the stub drops out. The little packet
         of replacement leads is
Somewhere I forget. I rummage in the dressing-table
         knick-knack drawer for a Biro
Pen I know is there from God-knows-when. It's actually a Bic.
         I start to write and find
It won't. I scribble nix until the vein gives ink. Where was I?
         'Temple, rock and cloud'—
Yes! I'd meant to look it up in Richard Verdi's book, and there
         it is—I'm typing this
In daylight now—'Even to the naked eye it is apparent that
         these rocks were painted

Over a layer of cloud and were added at a later stage,' he said
        in Carolyn Beamish's
Translation from the French. I take a magnifying glass to it
        to see if it is true.

It is. And still appears so, even to my naked eye, now I know
        it is, the brain translating
Eye to brain. I'm looking deep into the conjugated rock and
        cloud. But is the iffy overpainting
Deliberate? You never know with Poussin's sleight of hand.
        Look over to the left, below,
Behind, and there's a dome you didn't see before, and then,
        beyond, upon the distant
Skyline—it must be miles away!—a twin-towered structure
        looms enormously, although
From this far off it looks so small. And over to the right, there's
        more: turrets, palaces,
Magnificent establishments, the city going on in back much
        further, higher, deeper, greater than
You thought. Mindboggling prospect! What then lies
        immediately before our eyes?
'If this is our introduction to the city of Megara,' a tourist
        might enquire, 'where is
The monumental gate, the battlemented wall? We seem
        to have arrived at the periphery.'

Thinking architecture, wondering where to go next, I go for
        a walk to see what's

Going on in Hopefield. Significant progress. A white articulated
        lorry—LARSEN PILING—
Is parked at the site. They've replaced the chain-link with
        shuttered fencing and a gate.
I peep through a chink to see nine great big tall steel piles
        embedded in the excavation.
I think New York, the Chrysler and the Empire State, the
        bedrock layers of Manhattan schist,
Zigzag terrazzo on the lobby floor, marble fitments in
        the mezzanine, the terracotta veins
In my contemporaneous almost ninety-year-old onyx pencil.
        Look at it beside me
On the desk, and think, who might have picked it up in 1931
        to write some words, as I do now.

At last I'm on the threshold. Here lies what remains of Phocion,
        falsely condemned
By the Athenians, sentenced to drink the hemlock, his
        unburied body subsequently to be banished
To Megara, and burned at the border: the foreground, where
        his widow kneels to touch
The shadows of his ashes, not yet having gathered them.
        Her servant keeps lookout. Look
Again at the sunlit campus, people walking, talking,
        swimming, playing music, shooting,
Hitting the target again and again. They seem to cast no
        shadow. They are indifferent

To the exiles in the shadow of the oaks. As for you, you are
                  beyond the pale
Of the picture, immaterial to them who thrive in this Elysium.
                  Below the rock that veils
The cloud, it seems the city goes on living for the moment, or
                  for ever. I go on writing.

Gustave Caillebotte,
Paris Street, Rainy Day, 1877

after Francis Ponge, 'La pluie'

The rain, in the courtyard where I'm watching it come down,
        comes down at many
Different rates of knot. Its central zone is a finely woven
        curtain—sheer net, perhaps—
Thinly broken, relentless in its fall, but relatively slow,
        which must be down to the
Lightness and size of its droplets, an ongoing, frail
        precipitation, like real weather atomized.
Heavier and noisier the elemental drops that fall close
        to hand to the walls to
The left and right: here the calibre of grains of wheat, there
        plump as peas, elsewhere ample
Glassy marbles. Along window rail and sill the rain washes
        horizontally, while clinging to
Their undersides in rows of tetrahedral beads. According to
        the whole surface of a little
Zinc roof overhung by my lookout, it streams in a very fine
        sheet, shimmering on account of
The currents variously created by the imperceptible
        undulations, bumps and ripples of the metal
Blanketing; and from the adjoining gutter, where it moves
        reluctantly with all the force of

A low-gradient runnel, it suddenly releases its flow in a long,
                perfectly vertical, lazily braided
Thread to the ground where it shatters and spatters into
                brilliant glinting needles.
Each of its modes generates a particular tempo to which
                a particular sonority responds.
The whole ensemble pulses like a complicated, living
                mechanism, as precise as it is
Erratic, like a store of clocks whose springs depend on the
                weight of a given mass of
Constantly condensing vapour. The tinkling of vertical strings
                as they strike the ground; gutters
Going glug-glug; dings, dongs and tiny gongs; all resound and
                multiply in simultaneous concert,
By no means monotonous, and not without a certain fluid
                delicacy. And in due course, as
The springs run out of steam, some of the waterwheels go on
                operating, though more slowly,
And more slowly, until the mechanism ticks to a halt. Then
                the sun comes out once more
To wipe the slate clean; the whole brilliant apparatus
                evaporates—it has rained.

Nicolas Poussin,
Landscape with a Man Killed by a Snake, 1648

Never mind the death in the foreground, for months I've been
        pondering the miniature
Figures in the distance, composed of hardly more than a couple
        of strokes or dots
Of paint, more or less imperceptible at first viewing—figures
        that, once seen,
Exercise a gravitational pull out of all proportion to their actual
        size. I've been especially attracted
By the tiny pair—are they women, or men in togas, or, indeed,
        man and woman?—
Standing by the high farmstead in the upper left of the
        picture—there!—in a patch of sunlight.
Mere signs of figures that they are, we are free to speculate
        on what they might be
Up to, up there on the bluff. They could be us, out for a walk,
        discussing what
We see en route: peripatetic like the Ancient Greeks who liked
        to do philosophy
While strolling in the groves of academe, pointing to this and
        that from their high vantage point.

In any event the red and light blue of what they are wearing
        is electric; and as a consequence
We take cognizance of the slightly larger, darker red and blue
        walkers down by

The lakeside—in the gloom where the swimmers have thrown
        off their clothes.
So the figures begin to proliferate in twos and threes, little cells
        of people on the very
Verge of legibility, but never insignificant. As Jock McFadyen
        said, 'Painting can be
Symphonic—you've got everything from a sweeping brush
        to a No. 1 sable
With just two hairs. Like in an orchestra, you've got brass,
        woodwind, strings, and the guy
With the triangle going *ting!* It's all important.' Poussin liked
        to play with that kind of counterpoint.

We recognize it in his *Baptism* of 1642 where a beautiful
        shadow figure in a blue robe is
Visible over the Baptist's shoulder; then three men in togas
        at ease in a far meadow,
And a tiny couple to the left disappearing over the brow of
        a hill. In the *Marriage* of 1648,
Seen through a window immediately behind the bridegroom's
        head, a pair of inch-high figures
Hold colloquy in a narrow city alley—minuscule to the
        majuscule of the ceremony.
What a tableau they make, the two dozen or so participants
        in sumptuous array
Of blue, red, and yellow robes, recalling Félibien's observation,
        how Poussin
Would 'set out little models on a table, which he dressed
        in clothes so as to judge

The effect and disposition of all the bodies together'—the
        painter also thinking, in this instance,
Of wedding processions sculpted in marble on the sarcophagi
        of early Christian Rome.

Yesterday at Hazelbank a marble frieze or mountain range of
        cloud, opalescent at the edges,
Lay on the horizon. Lough water sparkled. And today is also a
        beautiful morning
For walking. We stop at the Hopefield site to see what's what,
        to find a great big
Four-foot-deep pit dug into it by the big yellow JCB that's in
        the middle of it.
We're looking it over through the security fencing when I say,
        'Look! Can you see
The cat?'—for three house martins have just landed not too far
        from it, beginning
To plunder the freshly-dug earth—and you say, 'Where?'
        and I say, 'Over there!'
But it's disappeared—a tabby, it was perfect camouflage against
        the mud—

Whereupon it reappears, quivering on the edge of the pit.
        Then, pounce!
The birds scatter, one of them too late. The cat pins it with
        a paw, then puts its mouth
To it. 'Landscape with a Bird Killed by a Cat,' you say. 'Yes,' I say,
        and think again

Of Poussin's painting, where the main event is not
                immediately discernible, but
Remains to be stumbled on in the shadows, our eye following
                the visible distress
Of the man running in the sunlit foreground, then the woman
                kneeling on the path,
Her widespread arms asking, 'What? Where?'—only then do
                we get to focus
On the strange entanglement of man and snake in the dark bed
                of the stream;
And we imagine Poussin with a little model of the *mise en scène*,
                figuring how best to drape
The body with the dummy snake, considering the twists and
                turns of its disposition.

Hence the zigzag path into the picture, and the correspondence
                of the minor to
The major figures. Look how the crawling posture of the body
                is echoed by the fisherman
Who hauls his net on this side of the lake, and further—
                out there, on the far, far side—
By one of two minuscule bathers, who has plunged his two
                arms into the water as if
Catching a fish with his bare hands, or picking up a stone.
                It's only then you notice
The little entourage off to the right on dry land, what seems
                to be a woman on a donkey

Preceded by two footmen, on a path to the sunlit city of Platonic
        cylinders and cubes, and we
Perceive again that other architectural configuration on the
        hilltop, made of blocks of light and shade.

And there's the pair of tiny people, one in red and one in blue,
        that might be you and me,
Except we're here, in Hopefield Avenue, on our routine journey
        to the Waterworks.
We stop for a moment at the House of Kids: there's the yellow
        toy dumper truck,
The green snake of the garden hose, etcetera, and a new
        addition, a male and female couple
Of garden gnomes, him taking a selfie with his arm around her,
        him in red, her in blue. We smile
And move on. We climb the embankment to the Upper Pond.
        There on the far side
Are the fishermen in jungle camouflage fatigues beside their
        little khaki tents,
Then the walkers, the dog walkers, bright sportswear, red, blue,
        yellow: people dotted
Poussin-like about the perimeter. A few paces on we stop,
        for there on the grass verge
Lies a three-foot-long pike, jaw agape, body glistening
        and fading in the late May sun.

Gerard Dillon,
Self Contained Flat, exhibited 1955

As in a medieval panel of the saint proceeding through the
      landscape of his miracles
Gerard Dillon is seen three times under various appearances
      in the same frame, here
Is Dillon in a blue fisherman's pullover walking in the door as
      skewed from the perspective
Of the wee hallway-cum-kitchen another door or is it the same
      door lies open to show
Dillon gardening on the garden path in denim dungarees as
      Dillon in the foreground in
A bold blue and white check shirt and red-trimmed light grey
      sports cardigan stands by a pine worktop
Emblazoned with the emblems of his trade: blowtorch, bottle
      of spirits, screwdriver, pliers,
As if to say fisherman gardener painter-decorator here I am this
      that and the other.

What great colours there are in this painting—the Cardinal or
      Chagall Red of the carpet
Corresponding to the red trim of the cardigan that
      complements the Green Carnation Green
Of Dillon's foreground face; the Madonna Blue of the raincoat
      hung on the yellow dresser,

Yellow that for Dillon stood for happiness, as in *The Yellow
           Bungalow*, Daffadowndilly Yellow
Of the single bed a naked figure occupies whatever she or he
           might represent
The colours of the rainbow as if to say Gauguin Chagall icon
           painter here I am this that and the other.

Basil Blackshaw,
Windows I–V, 2001

1

All these months I've been looking around for ways to describe
      the windows that would be
By definition to write about the windows or indeed around
      them: not so much to delineate
As to allow a little leeway as to what they mean that must
      include the shifting memories,
The unreliability of exactly when it was I first set eyes on them
      seventeen years ago—
Give or take a month or two—in the Ulster Museum. And were
      you there with me then?
I can't remember, nor can you when I ask. But we like to think
      of that first viewing
As by both of us, whether probable or possible we cannot tell
      in this long retrospect.
And as for the present moment, I've been writing 'windows'
      for all that they are not.

They are paintings of windows, each entitled *Window* followed
      by a Roman numeral,
Which we assume denotes the order in which they were
      painted. And dimly I remember
The 'window' adumbrated by Alberti in his *On Painting* (1435).
      I've just looked

For it online, and here it is: 'Let me tell you what I do when
          I am painting. First of all,
On the surface which I am going to paint, I draw a rectangle
          of whatever size I want,
Which I regard as an open window through which the subject
          to be painted is seen.'

    2

But what if the subject to be painted is a window? Interestingly
          we can see nothing
Through these painted windows, beyond the various shades
          of paint they're rendered in
Which might well represent the world beyond. Big pictures —
          measuring
Six feet by four or five except for number V, which is four
          by three — with horizontal glazing bars,
The paint consisting of near-monochromatic hues of grey,
          white, dun, grey-blue, khaki,
Muddied olive-grey, the dragged and scumbled paint spilling
          out from the ostensible glass
And over the edges of the painted window frame toward the
          frame of the painting,
The way light shimmers at the edges of an actual window given
          the conditions

Which are granted to the artist. They could be studio windows.
          As it happens,

Numbers *I* and *V* are both inscribed 'The Window where Neil
        Paints'—like a title scribbled almost
As an afterthought, but left unsigned, as are all the paintings,
        unless he signed them
On the back. Paintings of light, or paintings of paint for that
        matter, a record of the process,
Abstracted windows—homages, perhaps, to Mark Rothko—
        they still remind us
Of real windows, since everything we look at is conditioned
        by the eye of memory.

3

So I'm writing this in the parlour and I'm about to go and
        ask you for the umpteenth time
What you think about when you think of Blackshaw's *Windows*,
        when I spy you
Through the bay window tending to something in our
        minuscule front garden—tying
To its trellis an unruly tendril of the newly purchased sweet pea
        as it transpires, which
A week ago produced its first flower, a purple one. Today,
        finding it fully blown, you
Cut it to encourage growth as you'd been told. So now we're
        looking forward to
A bountiful array of colour: violet, royal blue, white, rose pink,
        lavender, magenta.

But never yellow; like the blue rose, the yellow sweet pea
        remains elusive.

Now the blinds are drawn in the bedroom bay window,
        we're talking by lamplight.
I shut my eyes the better to visualize *Windows* I and V,
        thinking how different they are
Though nominally the same 'Window where Neil Paints'—
        as if to say that there is always
Something else to see in everything we see, and that familiarity
        blinds us.
I open my eyes. And there, on the bedroom wall, I see
        Jim Allen's *The House with the Palm Trees,*
And I remember how its garden of sweet peas and roses
        was surrounded by barbed wire.

4

The next morning I take it down to the parlour and prop it on
        the back of the sofa
To look at it more closely, this lithograph I've had for forty years
        or so, given to me
By the artist because the house with the palm trees, otherwise
        33 University Road,
Was where I rented my first flat. The print depicts part of a
        terrace of Victorian houses
With big sash windows. Two of them mine, on the first floor.
        It was 1976 and I remember how

They'd tremble in the aftershock of the occasional nearby
                bomb, but not where I was
When they bombed The Club Bar on the opposite side
                of the road in May of that year.
So it's on my mind later that day when I meet Paul Nolan
                in the Linen Hall Library café.

There he is sitting at a table in the sunlight from one of the big
                first floor sash windows
Overlooking the City Hall. I join him, we get coffee and get
                to talk. 'The noise, the sudden
Plunge into darkness,' he said, 'everyone out of their seats,
                chairs and bar stools scattered,
Plaster falling off the ceiling, and the awareness that the one
                light source was the exit
To the entry and to safety. I followed a man who was covered
                in plaster and made it out.
Two people died that night, one Protestant, one Catholic.
                And I went on to a party.'

    5

These days of an afternoon I sometimes find myself in the
                bedroom lying gazing at
The ornamental plaster ceiling rose, imagining myself to see
                it from above, this great
Mappa Mundi circle of landscape under snow in high relief
                of valleys, mountains, clouds,

Sometimes thinking of the day that weeks after The Club Bar
        bombing, the ceiling of my bedroom—
Ornamental rose and all—collapsed with an almighty crash
        of inches-thick Victorian
Lath and plaster, as if it only then remembered the event.
        At the time I was in the kitchen
Cooking up a hangover fry. And still my memory of the bomb
        is blank. All I know is that I wasn't
There then, could have been, and here I am now, talking to Paul
        in the sunlight in the Linen Hall.

As for Blackshaw's *Windows*, Deirdre, we remember them
        forever in the changing light of
Fading in and out, and is that snow beyond the glass, or clouds
        that look like snow
Is on the way, that is the paint they're made of everything
        translucent not transparent.
You tell me again of those first-floor café windows you always
        like to look out from.
Tell me again of that man you once saw reading the paper about
        to walk into a lamppost
Until the old lady struggling with a shopping trolley knocked
        him off his stride.

Yves Klein,
IKB 79, 1959

'Blue are the shaded slopes of mountains and clouds'—
    a sentence drifted in from out of
Where I'm trying to remember, now I remember the far off
    muffled boom of
The White Mountain quarry that was decommissioned years
    ago, an echo of the echo
As a cloud of limestone elevated in the intervallic blue above
    the mountain.
Did I come across it in a book about Yves Klein? Lately I'd been
    looking into him,
And you could not think of Klein without thinking of blue,
    and seeing it
In some shape or shade or other hovering in the inward eye.
    As for *IKB 79*,
I've been asking you off and on for some months now when
    we might first
Have seen it where it hangs in the Tate Modern in London.

Isn't it strange, how we sometimes clearly remember our first
    viewing of a painting,
But rarely if ever what day it was, let alone the calendar date?
    We never kept
A journal. As it is, we don't even know the decade, and the
    memory of *IKB 79* floats free of

Everything that might have been that day, and is hence the very
icon of its being. All it is
Is nothing more than blue paint applied to a canvas-covered
panel some five feet by four,
One of some two hundred such monochrome paintings made
by Klein before he died
In 1962 from a hereditary heart condition, aged just thirty-four.
Klein had left these works
Untitled, but his widow posthumously numbered them *IKB 1*
to *IKB 194*, a sequence
Which did not reflect their chronological order, no doubt
because

Even she could not determine when each had been composed.
And likely even Yves Klein
Himself could not have done so, for all that he maintained that
each presented a completely
Different atmosphere: the painting was not what it looked like,
but the intensity of feeling
That had gone into it: the blue was a feeling blue. For all that,
I wonder what
Madame Klein would have felt as she numbered the panels,
and how the task was achieved.
How widely dispersed were the paintings? The acronym stood
for 'International Klein Blue',
Presuming some international notoriety; and, especially since
the death of their maker,

They had assumed something of the status of a holy relic.
        Did she view each of them in person,
Reliving the moment they had first come into being under
        her gaze?

In other words, did she remember them, and what else might
        have transpired that day?
Did she authenticate them by touch as well as sight? Klein
        had looked long and hard
For a suitable canvas before settling on a cotton sailcloth used
        for the canopies
Of Paris market stalls. He liked its artisan quality, its
        association with both sea and sky.
For him it evoked the blue of Nice, where he was born, the blue
        of the Côte d'Azur.
Each canvas was a unique textural field of nubs and bracks,
        tending to make each painting
Come out that little bit palpably different. Depending on
        the pressure of the roller, some panels
Looked thinly painted, or lush and velvety, the surfaces of
        others undulating, grooved or rutted.
'Though every moment in time has its unique quality,'
        said Klein,

'All can be absorbed by blue.' And again I imagine Madame
        Klein gazing at the icon,
Touching it, remembering, or struggling to remember. And
        here we are, remembering ourselves

Before it. Or rather, that was yesterday, and here I am, trying
        to pick up the thread
Of what it is that might transpire. Again I hear the muffled
        boom of the quarry, leading to the cloud
Of white dust, reminding me that Klein had visited Hiroshima
        in 1953. As he was being shown
Around the city he remarked on the beautiful, cloudless blue
        of the sky, and was told
That the atom bomb had been dropped out of such a sky on
        6th August, 1945. In that immaculate
Sky of 1953, the few relics of the city's most defining moment
        —that of its erasure—
Stood out clearly amidst the ongoing work of reconstruction:

The ruined dome of the once beautiful art deco Hiroshima
        Prefecture Industrial Promotion Hall,
Still left partly standing when all else around it had been
        levelled, had been preserved
As an admonitory, commemorative feature, as were the
        shadows imprinted on hard surfaces
By things and people vaporized by the explosion. Etched into
        the wood of an electric pole
Were the bold, serrated leaves of a *Fatsia Japonica*, which
        reminded Klein of reports he had heard
Of the patterns burned into the skin of some women, from
        the shapes of the flowers
On their kimonos. He learned that in the immediate aftermath
        of the explosion people

Supposed they had been the victims of a *Molotoffano*
hanakago — a 'Molotov flower basket',
The Japanese name for the self-scattering cluster-bomb known

To the Americans as a 'breadbasket'. When the full extent of
the devastation
Began to be realized, a rumour circulated that an aircraft had
dusted all of Hiroshima
With a special magnesium powder so fine as to be invisible,
which exploded like
A gigantic photographic flash when ignited by a spark from
an overhead power cable.
At the Red Cross Hospital word went around among the staff
that there must indeed
Have been something very peculiar about the bomb, because
on the third day
The second-in-command had descended to the basement and,
opening the vault
Where the X-ray plates were stored, found the whole stock
exposed as they lay. Only gradually
Did the truth emerge, and then it was not believed by many.

Klein's visit to Hiroshima was by the way. He had gone to Japan
principally to study judo.
He became an expert practitioner of the discipline, being
awarded the 4th dan black belt
On December 14th, 1953. He had long been fascinated by how
the body cuts a shape in space,

Leaving behind innumerable, invisible impressions of itself
           on the air. Although the principle of judo
Was not one of staccato aggression, but of flowing with things,
           Klein recognized that its repertoire
Of actions could be broken down into a series of pivotal
           moments. In his book *Les fondements du judo*,
Published in 1954, he analysed the syntax of judo movements
           in meticulous detail,
Accompanying them with hundreds of still photographs
           derived from film footage
Taken in Japan: illustrations of the importance of timing, of

Recognizing the split second when the opponent's equilibrium
           can be turned to disequilibrium,
His apparent greater strength to weakness. Learning to fall,
           one learned to overthrow. Gradually
Through practice and inner visualization, the most effective
           attitudes were remembered
By the body, so that its responses to attack became second
           nature. Klein was deeply affected by Hiroshima.
He paid homage to the ghostly presences of its atomic
           silhouettes in his imprint *Hiroshima*.
This was one of a series of '*Anthropométries*', made by spraying
           blue pigment
Around live models posed on a large sheet of white paper who,
           when they removed
Themselves, left behind a shadowy, retrospective choreography
           of body-shaped spaces

That recalled the faint impressions left by a person
          on a judo mat.

Another of the series was entitled *Humans Begin to Fly*. Shapes
          or shades of people apparently
Hovering in an indeterminate space above or below the actual
          painting surface.
Klein had always been fascinated by the concept of flight.
          'Today,' said Klein, 'the painter of space
Must actually go into space, but without aeroplane, parachute,
          or rocket. He must be
Capable of levitating.' From his judo experience, he believed
          that levitation—he liked
To think of it as a form of ascension, a victory over death—
          was indeed possible,
Through a regime of breathing exercises designed to free the
          body—physically, mentally,
And spiritually—from the constraints of weight. In November
          1960 Klein published
The photograph which became known as *The Leap into the Void*.

It appeared on a convincing replica—a fake—of the front page
          of the French journal *Dimanche*,
And showed Klein, dressed in a business suit, soaring into
          space just off the ledge
Of a mansard roof, his torso and head turned toward the sky,
          his arms flung outwards

In a theatrical facsimile of flight. The setting is a nondescript
        suburban Paris street,
Empty except for a man on a bicycle who has just passed by,
        his back to the viewer, oblivious
Like the figures in Bruegel's *Icarus*, to the marvellous event.
        When I first saw
A reproduction of *The Leap into the Void*, I was struck by the
        quotidian beauty of the scene,
The crooked kerbstones, the empty bus shelter, the tarred road
        patched and laddered with repair-work,
Light glinting off the leafy trees and the iron railings of
        a garden.

How wonderfully the cyclist defies gravity, how intricate
        are the folds and puckers of his overcoat,
Caught in mid-flap behind him! Klein's *Leap into the Void* might
        have been a camera trick,
But the street is miraculously real. The English title is a kind
        of shorthand. More accurately,
The photo bore the caption, *UNE HOMME DANS L'ESPACE!*
        Le peintre de l'espace se jette dans le vide!
Where *vide* bears slightly different connotations to 'void'.
        Vide is empty, space, vacuum, gap.
Optiquement vide, optically clear. *Parler dans le vide*, to waste
        one's breath. *Roulement à vide*, free-rolling.
Faire le vide dans son esprit, to make one's mind go blank.
        Different semantic implications.

So, pondering again the manifold uses of 'blue', I turn to
               William Gass, *On Being Blue*, and open it
At the first page to find the sentence I began this poem with.

Blue is indeed the colour of 'the shaded slopes of mountains
               and clouds, and so the constantly
Increasing emptiness of heaven, consequently the colour
               of everything that's empty.'
Regarder dans le vide, to stare into space. As for Yves Klein,
               through blue and beyond blue,
He felt himself 'grazed by the quivering of the absolute,
               the tangible representation of celestial space.'
As for me, it was one of those cloudless summer days when
               one can see for miles.
I'm lying on my back in the back garden of Mooreland Drive,
               gazing mesmerized into the blue
At the miles-high glittering speck of a jet plane and its contrail
               turning minute by minute
To fluff when *boom!* I looked east to the mountain a mile away
               to see nothing, when *boom!*
A minute later, another *boom!* Two-three minutes, another
               boom!

I looked west to the city centre three miles away to see cloud
               after cloud blossoming into the blue.
And so forth, and so on: after all these years from time to time
               the buried memory comes back

Out of the blue as it were. I never know the date, I must look
                for it online. Bloody Friday, 21st July 1972.
Grainy black-and-white, flickering dismembered shapes
                and shades of things
As mountain becomes cloud, and buildings rubble, cars
                and buses scrap, some of the dead
Have neither shape nor make to them, so mutilated, torn
                to pieces by the blast the

Body count was twice revised, from thirteen to eleven, down
                to nine.

The people who had set the bombs apologised in empty
                language.

Firemen shovelled into body bags the unspeakable remains
                of the day.

James Allen,
The House with the Palm Trees, c. 1979

The next morning I bring the Jim Allen down to the parlour
        once more to prop it on
The back of the sofa, pleased again by how the pale greens
        and the dark greens
Of the foliage stand out against the faded peachy pink of the
        fabric. And now
I'm looking at them, I see some yellow flowers among the red
        and white, for all
There was no yellow in my recollection. How could that be?
        I shut my eyes
And still I see them lavender and cream and violet, rose pink,
        never yellow
As the sweet pea never is. Was I thinking—am I thinking—
        of the garden in
The real world as it was three years before this print of it
        was made?
There's an area of what looks like freshly turned earth
        in the picture,
Which means the garden must have changed since I left
        the flat forever
In whatever year that was, though I believe for certain it
        preceded 1979.
For all that, perhaps my memory is plausible, and false,
        engendered by your tending

To the sweet pea—wishful thinking really. As Henri Bergson
        said, 'There is no perception
Which is not permeated with memories. But hence also springs
        every kind of illusion.'

Whatever the case—and 'The world,' said Wittgenstein,
        'is everything that is
The case'—the picture and my memory of what it represents
        are dwelling places.
It reminds me that it seems an age—what with this, that
        and the other,
Five sessions of radiotherapy among them—since we surveyed
        the Hopefield Avenue
Building site, now advertised as '9 two-bedroom apartments'.
        And we wonder
For the umpteenth time when Belfast people started to dwell
        in 'apartments'.
What happened to 'flat'? But no matter. The day has been
        showery, with windows
Of sunshine, one of which has just appeared, so off we go
        to view the progress
Of the new whatever you might call them. Significant
        development! There's a proper foundation,
Five courses of breezeblock laid flat on a ground floor plan,
        looking for all the world
Like a newly excavated Ancient Roman villa, were it not so
        pristine in appearance.
What a lovely oxymoron of a word is 'breezeblock', composed
        of airiness and solid mass

Conglomerate, from French *braise*, 'hot charcoal, embers',
        hence English 'breeze', fine cinders,
Clinker, coke, which when you add cement, become
        breezeblock. Which leads me to a 1950s builders'
Watchman's hut, whose denizen attends a brazier of glowing
        coke, and guards the new 'estate'—
A word derived from Latin *status*, 'where one stands', which also
        is the etymology of 'stanza'.

'Most words,' said the Society for Pure English, 'when first
        borrowed are *aliens*, but if they survive
They are generally accommodated to the language which
        borrows them, and they become *denizens*.
We left it there, meaning to continue to the Waterworks,
        but a navy blue cloud loomed from the mountain
To incline us homeward by Vancouver Drive and Kansas
        Avenue to Glandore, remarking
In passing how fresh and green were the leaves of the newly
        rinsed chestnut trees
On the corner of the Antrim Road. As we reach the porch
        of home the rain comes on,
Spattering the sweet pea. And now *The House with the Palm Trees*
        appears
In a different light. There's a nice palette of colours—shades
        of 1960s 'Neapolitan' ice cream
(Vanilla, strawberry, and chocolate) and sugared almonds
        (duck-egg blue, mint green, aqua)
Which, given the palm trees, give the scene an almost
        Californian, David Hockney look.

You notice things I'd never taken in, like the garden gate just
          that little bit out of synch with
Its hinges, that somehow goes with the casually arranged
          mismatched plant pots
And what you call the 'optimistic' trellis, since, like many such,
          it hasn't yet been
Wholly scaled by its climber, and maybe never will. And the
          upper storey with its five sash windows
In a row is like an Edward Hopper in the enigmatic outlook
          of their glass:
Are those shadows glimpses of the rooms within, or echoes
          of the sky this side of them?

'Is an indistinct photograph a picture of a person at all?'
          said Wittgenstein, 'Is it even always an advantage
To replace an indistinct picture by a sharp one? Isn't the
          indistinct one often exactly what we need?'
As for the palm trees, one on either side of the garden path,
          they make dramatic shadows nothing like
What I remember of them on the stucco render of the terrace —
          clear-cut spiky silhouettes
That look like, now I think of it (as I didn't then), the *Fatsia
          japonica* the old lady downstairs —
She whose garden it was — kept in her front window.
          Palm trees, garden, house plant, the very
House itself, all swept away. What is it, ten, twenty, thirty years
          since they demolished it, and built
A reproduction in its place, that now accommodates a
          First Trust bank. 33 University Road, Belfast.

You can look it up on Google Street View, as I did just now.
        I'm comparing like with not quite like,
The windows furnished with Victorian 'Greek' pediments that
        were never there in the first place.
How I loved that old dilapidated flat! And I its denizen at ease
        below the peeling ceiling rose,
Luxuriating in the bathroom with its emerald frog and
        water-lily 'shot silk' wallpaper, admiring
The blue birds anticlockwise spiralling around the interior
        of the toilet bowl.
And I loved the buzz of the one-bar electric heater as a bus
        or a truck passed by,
And I loved the big windows and whatever I could see through
        them, be it cloudy or clear,
And the way they trembled and thrilled to the sound of the
        world beyond.

Acknowledgements and Notes

My thanks, firstly, to Peter Fallon of The Gallery Press, who has been my steadfast editor for some thirty-five years, and without whom this book would not have been possible.

Thanks also to those who read and encouraged the work in progress: Jim Allen, Guinn Batten and Dillon Johnston, Terry and Tara Canning, Patricia Craig and Jeffrey Morgan, Theo Dorgan and Paula Meehan, Leontia Flynn, Tess Gallagher, Alan Gillis, Hammy Hamilton and Nóirín Ní Thuama, Kerry Hardie, Jeff Holdridge, Candide Jones, Amanda Keith, Stephen Kelly, John Kindness, Michael and Edna Longley, Alice Lyons, Jimmy McAleavey, Clement McAleer, Brian McAuley, Gail McConnell, Medbh McGuckian, Miriam McIlfatrick, Jeanne McNair, Úna Monaghan, Sinéad Morrissey, Paul Muldoon, Pádraigín Ní Uallacháin, Paul Nolan, Malachi O'Doherty and Maureen Boyle, Frank Ormsby, Glenn Patterson, Ian Sansom, John Waters; the members of the Belfast Writers' Group, and the Seamus Heaney Centre postgraduate poetry workshop.

I am grateful to the editors of the following journals, in which some of the poems were first published: Kevin Young (and Hannah Aizenman) at *The New Yorker*; Eavan Boland at *Poetry Ireland Review*; Alan Jenkins at *The Times Literary Supplement*; and Gerry Smyth at *The Irish Times*.

Special thanks to staff of the Cancer Centre at the Belfast City Hospital for their unfailing kindness and generosity.

page 10   'a handful of marble and porphyry chips': See T J Clark, 'At Dulwich: Poussin and Twombly', *London Review of Books*, 25 August 2011. This image was the inspiration for the whole poem, perhaps the whole series of poems. In any event Clark's writing, particularly his masterpiece *The Sight of Death: An Experiment in Art Writing* (Yale University Press, 2006) informed much of my writing, and I wish to acknowledge that considerable debt.

page 13   *Landscape with a Man Washing His Feet by a Fountain*: The description of the painting comes from Clark, 'The Special Motion of a Hand: Courbet and Poussin at the Met', *LRB*, 24 April 2008.

pages 31–32   'his complex stoop and stride': See Clark, *The Sight of Death*, p. 60.

page 33   '*minuzzoli di porfidi*': See Clark, *The Sight of Death*, p. 66.

page 34   *Patinir ou l'harmonie du monde*, Maurice Pons and André Barret (Éditions Robert Laffont, 1980).

page 38   'sub-cloud car': As described in Tom D Crouch, *Lighter Than Air: An Illustrated History of Balloons and Airships* (Johns Hopkins University Press, 2009).

page 40   Tony Swain: *Tony Swain: Narrative Deficiencies Throughout*, published on the occasion of the exhibition *Tony Swain: Drowned Dust, Sudden Word*, 19 April–1 July 2012, The Fruitmarket Gallery, Edinburgh.

page 46   'said Constable': In *Memoirs of the Life of John Constable*, C R Leslie (Phaidon Press, 1951).

page 49   Tom Lubbock: Tom Lubbock, *Great Works: 50 Paintings Explored* (Frances Lincoln, 2011).

page 57	*Landscape with a Man Killed by a Snake*: The description of the painting owes much to Clark, *The Sight of Death*.
page 58	Jock McFadyen: As quoted in *The Observer*, 26 May 2019. 'Baptism' … 'Marriage' … 'Félibien's observation': See Clark, *The Sight of Death*, p. 67; also Clark, 'Poussin the Unbeliever', in *Heaven on Earth: Painting and the Life to Come* (Thames & Hudson, 2018).
page 70	Yves Klein: Much of the writing about Klein has been reworked from the 'Feeling Blue' chapter in Ciaran Carson, *The Pen Friend* (Blackstaff Press, 2009).
page 78	William Gass: William H Gass, *On Being Blue: A Philosophical Inquiry* (NYRB Classics, 2014).
page 81	Henri Bergson: Henri Bergson, *Matter and Memory*, (George Allen & Co, 1912). Wittgenstein: Ludwig Wittgenstein, *Tractatus Logico-Philosophicus*, (Routledge, 2001).
page 83	Wittgenstein: Ludwig Wittgenstein, *Philosophical Investigations*, (Blackwell Publishers, 2001).